Dancing With Shadows

D1738451

Greyson Levi

Table of Contents

Her Name

I've always been sure that I'm alone in this world. I'm trapped in a boat with a hole in the bottom of it, the sea of depression slowly filling the space where Hope once sat. She was a beautiful travel mate. Her eyes were the grey where I lived when I taught myself that everything wasn't always black and white. Her hands had cradled mine even when they were trembling. Her arms were warm and fought the cold that was my daily dose of anxiety. Her smile promised that one day I'll learn to cope with the fact that we have been on this boat, in this sea, for years. I was almost sure that she was right. We'd been doing "fine" for so long. "Alright" for as long as I can remember. I thought what Hope and I had was strong. I thought our bond was thin and wispy but made of iron.

One day I woke up and reached for Hope, but the darkness enveloped me. I searched for Hope's trembling hand, but it didn't cradle mine back. Her warm arms didn't welcome my cold body, and my anxiety was beginning to creep down my spine. She was just gone, or had I managed to push her away in my slumber? I was left adrift and searching. I was held by fear and carried by depression. I held on to prayers that I didn't have faith in. Maybe she'll come back; maybe she'll miss my trembling hands, my cold body, the way I delved into her grey irises. Maybe she would miss pulling me back into our boat when the sea was roaring

1

at me. Maybe she will want to help me patch up the holes. Maybe she will.... Or maybe she will let nature take its course. Either way, she better make a decision soon. Before the water takes her place in our boat.

19 January 2018

The Promise

There is so much that I wish I trusted you enough to tell you.

Like how I thought your smile for me was the only thing that was able to pull me out from behind the aquarium wall where I watched the world around me swim free. How speaking to you made my heart soar like no chains were shackling it to a sinking ship.

Your voice, I wish I could put into words how it made me feel when you sang. It was like being sprayed with a water gun on a hot day. Every single time your ballad started, it was shocking and soothing. It was analgesic for the wounds my mind had inflicted upon itself throughout the day.

Holding you, hugging you, touching you was the light. The light that shined into the precipice where my psyche sometimes vacations. The place so deep into myself that nobody dares to visit, not even god.

Somehow, you got through, and you pulled me through the darkness until that space finally became colors again. Brilliant colors that even when I close my eyes, there is no darkness. I'm floating when I'm with you. Escalating sky-high, limitless, nothing but an array of colors ready and willing for me to explore.

But then you let go of me. With no promises to hold on again, the light slowly dims, releasing me back into the trusting arms of darkness that promises never to release me. It says, "I never should have let you go to begin with. The light... The colors... The freedom was too much for you."

Feeling empty-handed, I shudder and embrace the solitude. The only thing that has promised never to abandon me. Because it promised... And it meant it.

16 June 2019

Believe It

He looks at himself through a splintering mirror. His red eyes are burning, and his lashes are heavy with the latest anxiety attack. His reflection is so violently different than what he knows he looks like. Where he once saw a meticulously coifed crown, he sees disheveled tangles. His once soulful eyes have been stripped of their light. His warm brown skin is now dry and tallied. This unfamiliar skin wears gashes where his feelings of weakness and insecurity try to claw their way out. He'd wanted to help them escape by highlighting an exit. A red flashing, puckering exit.

He drops the sharp highlighter on the bathroom floor. War-torn and ragged, but finally strong enough to let it go. He falls to his knees beside it. The foggy mirror reflecting his hell is the only company he has. He looks into the eyes of the reflection that he doesn't recognize. His tears are refugees, paying homage to the battle barely won. His brain is messy with remnants of an internal war. He collects his thoughts as sacrificed warriors drip from his wrists. Collateral to appease his suffering, to lower the weapons that his trauma has raised against its host. He searches for an anthem to celebrate this win. He searches for the words to boost the morale of the fighters he has left.

Words he desperately needs to believe.

He says, "I am not broken. I am not defeated. I did not give up. I am not what I see in front of me. I reflect the brightest side of the things I've been through. I am the best result of the tragedies in my life. I am choosing to live."

He repeats the mantra to himself. Each time louder than the last until he stands to his feet.

He looks at his face. He recognizes it in the mirror. It is the Brave face he puts on whenever he goes in public. The same face he puts on for his friends and family. The face of deceit. The face that people will never know dawns war-paint when he is alone.

He says the words one last time. Picks up his highlighter, and puts it in the medicine cabinet. He turns his back and walks away, leaving a single lonely phrase behind that destroys the effort that his affirmations had begun.

"Maybe one day, I'll believe it."

16 October 2019

When I Say I'm Okay

When I say I'm okay, what I really mean is that I'm used to this shit.

When I say I'm okay, it means that I'm in my natural state of discomfort.

When I say I'm okay it means that my brain is a prison. My mind, a raging tornado banging itself against each bar on every rotation.

When I say I'm okay, it means that no matter how much I want you to understand me, you likely never will.

When I say I'm okay, I don't expect you to be able to help me.

When I say I'm okay, sometimes that's all that is left of my crumbling heart. The words "not" and "help" left to sacrifice themselves as martyrs.

When I say I'm okay, I'm begging you to see that I'm lying, but I'm urging you not to ask if I'm sure.

When I say I'm okay, it translates to "I'm fucking terrified."

When I say I'm okay, it means that my addiction is hovering in my peripheral, always letting me know that she's an option.

When I say I'm okay, she wants to cradle me and tell me that she will always be there for me. She says she can feel my pain even when the people I love the most refuse to acknowledge it. Her hands comfort mine, reaching for the very wrist she will try to use to dissect my flesh.

When I say I'm okay, I really mean that she whispers to me. She promises that she can detox my body from the anxiety and depression that parades like bulls through my blood.

Can't you see her? She is beautiful. Reliable. Honest. She loves me fully and toxically.

When I say I'm okay, the lie spills out as easily as her sweet song of euphoria. She sings that she wants me more than anyone else in the world.

When I say I'm okay, I'm telling you that she is serenading me with the sharpest tongue, and I want to be licked.

When I say I'm okay, I'm begging myself not to be ashamed of wanting to swim out to that siren's call.

When I say I'm okay, I'm resisting her one more time.

12 December 2020

Thoughts The Night Tried To Keep

The crazy thing about disregarding the past and focusing on the present is that the present becomes the past the moment it's over. You realize everything is fleeting. Sure, Sorrow only lasts for the night. Perhaps we can try to sleep it off, but the worst part of a broken heart is waking up.

28 September 2021

When You Left

When you left, you forgot to pack the loneliness and guilt as you walked out the door.

You left behind shattered emotions and mixed feelings. They'll be waiting for you when we meet again.

21 November 2021

Give Me Love

Love me how one loves a good book or how you love a Halloween decoration. Love me how you love the tiny sample spoons at Baskin Robbins. Love me without rhyme, reason, or commitment. Love me purely and without presumption. Love me, and do not hope that I'd be much more than all that I am.

1 May 2022

Ode To The Love Maker

This is an ode to the Love Maker. The Magician and The Sorceress. The Rootworker and The Priestess. The House Builder and The Homemaker. The Pillar Shaker and The Column Stacker. The Hand Holder and The Foot Stomper. The Comedian and The Critic.

The Alchemist, she who manufactures love through remnants left behind from childhood. Dearest Love Maker, has adulthood shown you healthy love?

This is an ode to the Love Maker. The one who has been broke and broke in but never broken. The potter who glued, casted, and molded their hearts back together, the cracks sparkling with flecks of golden wisdom. Brilliance shines so that their new love can see the lessons that the old one taught them. This is an ode to the Love Maker. The Mother and The Daughter. The Elder and The Child. The Divine Queen. I wish to understand the beauty of who you are.

20 June 2022

Just A Guy With A Lot Of Feelings

I'm not a love poet, but if you're reading this, it's because I've mustered up the guts to tell you how I feel.

I'm not a love poet, so don't judge me too harshly. My poems have been the remnants of mania and depression, coated with self-loathing and riddled with thoughts of suicide. I haven't been able to write poetry like that lately. You're my balm, my salve, my cure-all for the wounds my mind has created.

I'm not gonna say any corny shit like "you make me want to be a better man" or anything because I'm not a love poet, but if I were to write a poem about love, that poem would be about you.

The poem would be about how you swept into my life like a hurricane. You shook everything up and created messes in every room that my OCD brain doesn't know how to fix. You left your makeup on the counter of my frontal lobe. Kicked your shoes off and left them in the middle of the floor on my occipital. Rummaged through the closet of my cerebellum, and spilled your name all over my cerebral cortex. My brain is messy with thoughts of you and I wouldn't dream of cleaning it up.

The poem would be about how when you're asleep, I sketch the outline of your face with my mind. I paint you in technicolor, in greens and blues and firey reds. When you're sad, I paint you in watercolors, and when you're mad, I sketch you with hard lines. I make murals of your body with tiny shards of tile from all the pieces that you claim are broken; I can see the beauty in the cracks in your armor.

The poem would be about how timeless our souls are. How I look into your icy eyes and I can see the last 3 lifetimes we spent together and the next 50 years of this life with you. I'd write about the time when we separated 2 lifetimes ago. I was going to war and didn't want you to have to wait for me, and I died with your name on my lips, your image in my mind, and memories of our love grasped in my palm. I would write about how I was a Viking and you were my enemy. You shot the arrow that impaled me but held eye contact with me as I lay dying. My final breath was dedicated to you. See, we have always fought wars that weren't ours at the expense of ourselves. The idea of forever with you has always been collateral damage.

If I were a love poet I'd write about the song that your heart sings to mine. I'd write about how your melody vibrates through my bones, your chorus ricochets through chakra points. I can hear your lyrics with my id.

If I were a love poet, I'd write about how I want you to be my forever. I'd write about how it's your hands that I want to be holding when the world falls apart. With your cold hands in my warm ones, we will create tornadoes and hurricanes and comfort each other through the storms. I'd write about how I love you.

But I'm not a love poet, I'm just a guy with a lot of feelings.

25 December 2022

Slow Fall

Slowly. We fell in love slowly. We fell in love slowly over dirty jokes about lemon trees, sarcasm, and our appreciation for our ability to cry again. I kissed you on a three-count in my head after watching an episode of your favorite show. My hands danced across the skin along your abdomen, and my fingertips sang as they lightly kissed their way down your collarbone. My lips longed to do the same. When our lips finally danced, the tango was beautifully awkward. My blood sang and my heart belted a tune Mariah Carey would be proud of.

26 March 2023

On Worship

I think I fell in love with you the first time I heard you laugh. It was obnoxious and vibrated through the air, shaking up the settling dust. I witnessed the unsettling through the rays of your smile. It agitated me. Made me feel something I'd never felt before. At that moment, I suddenly realized you. So, does that make you my epiphany?

You became the book I couldn't wait to read but dreaded the coming of the ending.

You became my new religion and the confirmation that there is a god and his goddess of a daughter walks on earth. I wanted everyone and no one else to see your glory.

28 May 2023

The First Time

The first time I touched you, it was barely a whisper. Barely a caress, but the hair on your arms stood on end. Seemed they'd reached for me as if anticipating my departure, never knowing you'd be the one to walk away.

13 July 2023

Closed Curtain

If you keep pretending to love me, I promise you can come back. If you make no promises and tell me no lies, will you come and hold me? Will you tell me I don't need you? That I'm strong enough to be without you? That I'm not lonely, I'm just alone? Maybe I'll believe it coming from your mouth; hell, I believed everything else.

I know you didn't mean to hurt me. That you really do love me. I know that it was a few mistakes and you didn't mean to lie. Can you just put on a show this last time? I won't ask again. One last kiss, a last caress. One final act before the curtains close.

24 September 2023

Haunting You

When you broke my heart for the second time, I carefully packed your belongings and set them at the front door. I told you I hope you get everything you deserve in this life, and I meant that... sort of. I meant that I hope I become your personal urban legend. I hope that when you think about me in the dark, the shadow in the corner of your room is my exact image. I hope that when you say my name, a memory of how I looked between your legs flashes back at you in your memory. I hope that when you are your happiest and most content, you can feel my hand on your shoulder. Can I be your ghost?

24 September 2023

Find Me

My hands envelop yours as we settle yet another kiss. I curse the very oxygen that I need to pull away from you.

"I knew it would be like this." You whisper.

"You knew what would be like what?" I ask, incapable of severing the smile from my lips.

"I knew I'd fall in love with you like this. I think I'll love you forever."

Your answer is full of so much conviction that I almost think it's true. You hold such power in your touch and in the breaths that still caress my lips that I'm almost sure the universe will bend to your will.

I've known this tightening in my chest before. This vibration of nerve endings, this spinning in my head like I've inhaled too much helium. I'm familiar with it. Maybe not quite to this degree, but I still remember the echoing, mournful apparition that is Love.

She is a slippery bedfellow. There one day and packing up for a long vacation the next. I miss her every time she leaves. And like the enabler that I am, I always turn down the bedding and welcome her in.

So I kiss you again and shatter your illusion of forever with the feather light touch of truth.

"I will love you until I can't anymore." My answer etches lines of worry upon your brow, and my knees buckle when I feel your heart drop.

"And how long will that be?" You ask, the chill of distance cooling the palms your hands once took shelter in.

"I will love you until the moment our hearts stop beating in tandem. I will love you until I've lived in every corner of your soul. I will love you until there is nothing else to fight for and nothing left to defend. I will love you until my will chokes out its final gasp. I'll love you when I hate you and you hate me. I'll love you long after this version of you is gone. Long after you no longer need today to get by, and we have slipped through your memory. I'll carry this version of who we are in my memories.

Perhaps someday we'll stop loving each other. Maybe Love will slip out of the door with everything but her picture book packed. Maybe we'll never see her again. Maybe we will be left with fading sepia photos of Love as we know her now, and when I look back over these photos, I'll find you there. Hidden in Love's eyes. Maybe you'll look back and find me.

26 January 2024

I Hate Her

I hate her because she is everything I want to possess. Everything I want to own. EverythingI want to be, to shrug into and feel comfortable in my skin. She is everything I want in my bed and in my body, decorating my skin and living therein. I hate her and love her cause she's everything I could have been. I mean everything I *should* have been.

She is divinity and femininity, and though I have moments when I can relate to her, I can never be her. I cannot twist and contort her mind to fit in my body. Perhaps I can fit into hers.

3 February 2024

Under Your Skin

Touch me, and let me exist only where my flesh meets yours. Allow me to be only as this spark of electrons, only this second in time. Look into me and see nothing but this tiny room of desire. Pay no attention to the ominous halls and locked doors. Touch your tongue to mine. Let me feel everything and nothing at all. Break me open on the canvas of your sheets. Fill me with oblivion and be the vessel that I empty my grief into. Know all of my body but ask nothing of my mind and heart. And tomorrow when your soul is stained with my sadness, know that I'm sorry that I didn't care. Know that I took everything that you didn't know you offered. Know that you will be addicted to the pain I've poured into you. And know that I'll be hoping for and dreading the next time we'll need each other.

23 April 2024

Escapism

I've always been a sucker for escapism. I fall in love with characters in books, act as the voyeur to television shows, and slide my unheard commentary between those of podcasters.

I've always existed to bear witness. Always happy to cheer everyone else on from the sidelines. It's my privilege to be your harbinger. I've always been the lucky one to live many lives while curled up in my recliner. Having real feelings about fictional things.

But holding your hand is the realest thing I've ever done. My reality doesn't seem quite so bleak when I'm near you. And although sometimes you choose to escape into movies and books and TV shows with me, I revel in the story between your pages.

Can I read your text?

Dance through your literary genius?

Tell me what scares you so I can absorb your thrillers.

Can I run my fingers across your poetic prose?

Exist in your biography?

Can you tell me about your first loves? Can I write a romance with you?

Can I crack the spine on the stories you've never let another read?

Can I escape into reality with you?

You know I'm a sucker for escapism.

13 May 2024

Author's Note

Dear Reader,

Thank you for reading my recounting of journeys of the heart, anxiety, depression, and coping. My poetry has been a place where I've worked through some pretty dark times. My deepest desire is that someone reads and can find something beautiful. I also hope that you find something relatable.

This publishing process has been my own manifestation come true. It has been my mantra. I've used it as a way of telling myself that I am worthy to be heard, and that my words can and has touched someone. Your story and your words can make a difference. Please keep writing, keep reading, keep living. Much love!

-Greyson L.

Made in the USA
Las Vegas, NV
27 October 2024

10058994R00017